Reclaiming Womanhood

Lyrica Solomon, MFT

Copyright © 2021 by Reclaiming Womanhood, LLC

All rights reserved. No part of this book may be reproduced or used in any manner without written permission of the copyright owner except for the use of quotations in a book review. For more information address: reclaimingwomanhoodllc@gmail.com

This book is dedicated to the woman who has been sexually assaulted. There is abundant life, in Christ, after assault.

Acknowledgements

First and foremost, I would like to thank God for giving me this book to write, the victory over my trauma, and the wherewithal to see this process through. Without Him, I would not have made it this far.

I also want to thank:

My grandmother, for being a praying woman.

My mother.

My mentors Davilyn, Nikki, Kimberly, Bola, and Abriel.

My friends Cindy and Kateva.

My motivator Steve, for pushing me on those days when I wanted to quit.

The men and women who offered their perspectives for this book.

My assailants, for giving me my story.

All those who believed in me.

CONTENTS

Introduction 1

Chapter 1: What We Have Come to Know About Women 5

Chapter 2: The Culture of Secrecy 19

Chapter 3: No Choice, No Voice 31

Chapter 4: Don't Touch Me 47

Chapter 5: Leverage 66

Chapter 6: Who Was I Without My Pain? 83

Chapter 7: A Flame in the Closet 100

Chapter 8: What it Means to be a Woman 116

Introduction

You arrive home one day to find a package on your doorstep. You inspect the package: shake it, feel for its weight, and listen for its contents. Upon determining that it's not a safety hazard, you take the package into your home. You open it up to find an object that you have never seen before. It appears to be an appliance of some sort that is used for something, but you don't know what for. You search the rest of the box and find a slip of paper that reads, "Call the manufacturer if you have any questions about the product". You decide to ignore the instructions and try to find information about this product on Google. You image search it and find nothing. You call up some friends and send them pictures, and they have no clue what this appliance is. So, you give in and you call the number on the slip of paper. The manufacturer explains what the appliance is and what it is to be used for. Wow.

How easy was that and how much more time could have been saved if you would have followed the instructions first?!

Now, let's take a step back and look at a much bigger picture. The most important thing about this scenario was knowing who the manufacturer was and having access to them. Without this information, you are left to your own demise to figure out how this appliance works. Sadly, I feel like this is what happens with us women. We run to Google, friends, family, drugs, alcohol, money, sex, etc to try to figure out who we are and what we are created for before we run to the one who created us, God. I am guilty. This woman was me. I didn't know any better. No one ever explained to me, at an early age, the importance of seeking God and allowing Him to define me. Because I lacked that foundation in God, it left me open to finding my value and defining my womanhood by any and everything that came my way. Step by step, and bit by bit, I was slowly being robbed of my original design in womanhood that God created me to be in.

Lyrica Solomon, MFT

The word *reclaim* means to retrieve or recover something previously lost, given, or paid. Throughout this book, I seek to explain how I fell away from my original design as a woman and how I was able to recover my true essence of womanhood in God. Let me be very candid here: the devil wants to attack your identity as a child of God and as a woman, and this isn't some recent development. An attack on your identity will have you wondering who you are. If you don't know who you are, you don't know your purpose. If you don't know your purpose, you cannot live the life that God has called you to and glorify Him. However, if you are aware of how the enemy moves, he can't take anything from you. This book is written to shed light on the tactics of the enemy so that you can live your life free from his grasp and step into your *true* identity as a woman of God. This book will challenge you to be self-reflective, vulnerable, and honest. These three things are key to achieving healing and wholeness through your relationship with Christ.

I know many of you, who are reading this book, probably share similar experiences with me. You may be wondering if there is hope for you after all you have been through as a woman and after all that you feel has been taken from you. Allow me to be a living example and tell you that *there is hope for you*. God not only wants to reveal to you *His* unique design for your womanhood in the kingdom of God, but He wants for you to live it, too.

CHAPTER 1

What We Have Come to Know About Women

I want you to take a second to think about the most important woman in your life right now. What qualities come to mind when you think about her? What makes her the woman that she is? I can almost bet that things like caring, loving, kind, selfless, motherly, etc come to mind. This is usually the typical answer that you would receive to a question of this nature. Yes, this description is great, but it doesn't paint the entire picture. I believe that in order to get a more accurate picture of how women are viewed, we must take a look at our society. Why? Because whether we want to admit it or not, mainstream opinion influences our viewpoint on everything. So, the question now becomes, "How does society view women?".

A Social Construct

A lot of what we have come to know about women is a social construct. A social construct is an idea that has been created and accepted by the people in a society. So, what image has our present society created about women that we have accepted? For the sake of this conversation, I have listed three categories that I feel encompass society's viewpoint of women. This viewpoint is not meant to be an "end all, be all" portrayal of women, but has been a recurring theme in my findings. Let's take a look.

Inferior

Inferior to who? Men. Many of you may have read the word "inferior" and cringed a little on the inside. I get it, we have made great strides at achieving equality across the gender board. However, this narrative is rooted in a long history of women fighting for equal rights in our country. Just because some numbers change in a person's salary, does not mean it addresses the mindsets of people about women. I'm sure some of you can attest to that.

Well, what does this look like? You have a successful woman who is the boss of a Fortune 100 company. Before her first day of work, she is concerned about what to wear, how to wear her hair, and how to act. Why? Because all of these could potentially influence the way that people view her at the company. If she is too nice, she will be viewed as a pushover. If she dresses too "cute", then she is trying to be promiscuous. If she wears her hair down, she's less likely to be taken seriously. This list goes on. Why do women have to prep themselves in this way just to be looked at as equal or to show their credibility? Because even though times have changed, mindsets have not. It is a sad reality. This mindset is not only seen in the occupational sense, but bleeds into the interpersonal relationships that women are involved in on a daily basis.

Emotional

From a very early age, women are given permission to show emotions. We are at liberty to feel what we feel and not be reprimanded for it. While our counterparts, men, are told to "stop crying before they are given something to cry about". As a result of this dynamic, women *tend* to be more in tune with what they are feeling and tend to be more expressive. With all their glory, our emotions can lead us to do some pretty irrational things. That's when we hear things like, "Man, you trippin'", "You doing too much", "Why you acting like that", "Get out of your feelings". Now, don't misinterpret what I am saying. I am not saying that having emotions or being emotional is wrong or a bad thing. I am simply stating that our reactions or responses to our feelings are not always the best. That goes for the entire human race, not just women. Think about how often you see a woman "acting out" or being "emotional" in the media. Let's take a reality television show: the first one that comes to your mind. Do a google search for "fights on _____", and fill in the blank with the tv show you thought of. Who comes up in the search for you? For me, women. Things like this communicate that women are messy, that women are bad with managing their emotions, and that women aren't mature enough to have a conversation without resulting to violence. Believe it or not, these subliminal messages are influencing not only how the world views women, but how women view themselves.

Object

If you have ever heard of the statement, "sex sells", it was probably a statement about women. Take a moment to think about all of the advertisements that you have ever seen. I can think of a few specific commercials where a woman is "washing" a car in a very sexual nature. What is this commercial advertising? A car? Absolutely not. The commercial is for a burger. Why does a woman need to portray herself in this way to sell a burger? Clearly, the marketing experts have figured out what catches the eye of the audience and it seems to be working. But why do we tend to drift toward things that have this sexual undertone? I don't even know where to begin to answer this question. However, what I do know is that our little girls, cousins, nieces, etc are absorbing these images of women into their psyches. What does this type of marketing communicate to a little girl about the way that she is supposed to carry herself?

Reflections

With taking time out to examine my upbringing and even the more recent happenings in my life, I have fallen upon some pretty harsh truths about the way these things have affected me. First and foremost, these were things that were taken on unconsciously over several years of being fed these types of things through my ear and eye gates. Somewhere along the line it registered in my mind that women had to be sexual in order to be valued or to get attention. This was my harsh truth. I have countless memories of little incidents that have happened in my life that made me feel so little. I had one guy hit me so hard on my butt that it lifted me off the ground. This same guy told my best friend that he would have sex with me so hard that my eyes would pop out of my head. I literally remember saying to myself in this moment, "I am a walking piece of meat". That's what I felt like. I felt like men only looked at me as something to receive sexual pleasure from.

I want to challenge all of you who are reading this to do a deep reflection of your past. Think about the things I have talked about and how those things have shaped who you are. I will insert some questions to prompt your self-reflection:

- How has the way society views women affected the way that I view myself?
- Have I found myself feeling pressured to "fit in" with what society says about women?
- In what ways do I seek validation? What makes me feel good about myself?
- What rules have I unconsciously lived by due to outside influences?

Lord, I pray that you expose things about my past that need to be addressed and any ungodly beliefs that I have about myself. Lord, perform an autopsy on me and take out anything that is not like you and pour into me all things that are of your Spirit. In Jesus' name, Amen.

Journal

Journal

Journal

Journal

Journal

Journal

CHAPTER 2

The Culture of Secrecy

"What's done in the dark, comes to the light."

There was a time that I was not privy to how my upbringing affected the woman that I am today. However, as I have gotten older, I have become more aware of myself. I am learning that every experience that I had, as a child, has in some way shaped how I view the world and interact with it. Some of those experiences include who raised me, my childhood friends, the schools I attended, and a multitude of other things. Of these experiences, I want to take some time to talk about how sex was viewed in my household while I was growing up.

The "Big" Secret

While in graduate school, I took a class called "Couples and Sex Therapy". One of my assignments for this class was to keep a journal. Amongst the journal prompts was a question that required me to think back to my first sexual experience. This sexual experience could have been something I experienced or something that I witnessed. By answering this journal prompt, I came to a few conclusions about what my family believed about sex.

My very first sexual experience dates back to when I was about six years old. Like any child at that age, I was very curious. I remember playing in the house one day and my mother gave me an instruction, "Do not come into my room". I agreed to follow her instructions, but as time passed, I became interested in what was going on in the room. About twenty minutes went by and I couldn't resist anymore. So, I went to my mother's bedroom door and quietly peeked in. You guessed it, my mother was having sex. I'm not sure how long I stood in the doorway or if I even knew what was going on. All that I knew was that my mom did not want me to know what she was doing and that she wanted to keep me from witnessing it. Subconsciously, what got processed in my six-year-old mind was this: the act that my mother was doing (that I would later come to understand as sex) was something you did behind closed doors so that no one would see and so that no one would know that you were doing it. In essence, sex was supposed to be kept a secret. As I got older, I began to display actions that fell in line with this "sex is a secret" mind frame. Every sexual encounter that I had from that point moving forward, I told no one. We never talked about sex in my household when I was growing up. I felt like I had no space to open up a conversation about sex, so I just kept it to myself.

Reflections

I think it is very important for conversations about sex to take place in our homes. This is why I want to encourage all families to have age-appropriate conversations about sex. It is important for the development of your child(ren). If you don't talk about it with them, they will more than likely hear about it from someone who doesn't have much experience (probably a peer). At this point, your child is receiving information about sex from a child that is their age. How reliable is that information? I don't think I have to answer that question for you to get the point. Allow my story to be an example of what could happen if you don't have these conversations with your children.

I can't help but wonder how different my life would have turned out if sex wasn't such a secret in my family. This seed of "sex is a secret" got planted and took root in many areas of my life in my early adult years. I get into this in a little more detail in the next chapter. With that being said, I leave you with some questions for reflection:

- How was sex viewed in my household growing up?
- How has this view of sex impacted who I am as a woman?
- Does my view of sex need some adjustments?
- What does God say about sex?

Lyrica Solomon, MFT

Lord, I pray that I open my heart to you. I pray that you search me and lead me to those things in me that are not like you so that I can submit them to you. In Jesus' name I pray, Amen.

Journal

Journal

Journal

Journal

Journal

Journal

Journal

CHAPTER 3

No Choice, No Voice

Choice. The act of selecting or making a decision when faced with two or more possibilities.

Making choices is at the basis of our human existence. We *have* to make choices. Every day we are met with a myriad of decisions to make. What time will I choose to set my alarm? What will I choose to wear today? What hairstyle will I choose to wear? What food will I choose to eat? Who will I choose to hang out with? Sounds pretty simple, right? Not entirely. For those of us who have experienced sexual assault, we were not awarded this luxury. Being sexually assaulted takes your choice away from you. The person who offends you, ultimately, decides that your wants/desires don't matter and makes the decision to push their own, selfish agenda, even if you have told them "no". In this chapter, I break down multiple experiences where I was not awarded the privilege to make a choice.

Incest

Let's take a second and address the topic at hand: incest. Before the age of twelve, I experienced some form of sexual assault with five different family members. I often ask myself why it is that ninety-three percent of sexual assault cases are committed by someone that the victim knows. Of that ninety-three percent, thirty-four percent are by family members (Department of Justice). Upon further investigation and becoming curious about my own healing, I have discovered that those that tend to be perpetrators have more than likely been victims of sexual assault at some point in their own lives. What is wrong with this picture? Generation to generation, these unhealthy patterns of relating are being passed down and are going completely unaddressed. How do we stop this vicious generational curse and cycle?

1. Spiritual warfare. Generational curses are nothing to be played with. These entities cannot be fought within your own strength. You need the power of the blood of Jesus and deliverance to break these curses off of your bloodline. I always think of the scripture from the book of Ephesians, "For we do not wrestle against flesh-and-blood enemies, but against evil rulers and authorities of the unseen world, against mighty powers in this dark world, and against evil spirits in the heavenly places" (chapter 6, verse 12, NLT). In other words, our struggle is not with the things and the people that we can see, but with those things that are unseen and evil spirits. Any type of sexual abuse, molestation, or assault comes with a spirit. That spirit has to be addressed and cast out of your life and family.

2. Speak up. We have to speak up about our experiences and make room for others to share, as well. You will be surprised at how your confession encourages someone else to speak up about what they have been through, too. These

things continue to run rampant in our family line because we don't speak about them. Let's speak up.

3. Changing the narrative. The narrative has been that touching on your family members is okay, and not only is it okay, but you are not supposed to say anything about it. THIS STOPS NOW. We have to start asserting our viewpoint about sexual assault within the family: it is wrong! It is not okay. We can no longer allow people to walk around thinking that everything is sunshine and rainbows when it comes to this topic. It's time to change the narrative.

Homosexuality

Underneath this category of family sexual assault, I have to address homosexuality. I am a firm believer in the sentiment that if a door is opened prematurely, that it exposes a person to things that they should not be exposed to. The door to sex was opened way too early for me. Because I was prematurely exposed to things that I shouldn't have been exposed to, nothing was off limits for me. I was exploring any and everything and no one knew about it. Two of my experiences were with females. As a result of these experiences, I often found myself questioning my sexuality and sexual orientation. I would ask myself questions like, "Well, if I let those things happen, does that mean that I'm bisexual or homosexual"? The devil wants you to say yes to this question, but let me be the one to put those wonderings and those whispers to rest. No ma'am, that does not mean that you are bisexual or homosexual. I will not allow the enemy to toy with your identity any longer. You were created to be with a man, love a man, and be attracted to a man. Be free from that mindset and be healed.

Rape

In my sophomore year of college, I met this football player. I'm not even sure how we got connected. It was Thanksgiving break of 2013. I was bored, so I hit Billy up. Billy invited me over for "Netflix and chill" and I knew what this insinuated. So, I let Billy know that I did not want to have sex and that I just wanted to watch movies. That was the agreement we made before I went over there, and Billy agreed. So, Billy came to get me and we went to his place. I remember that I felt uncomfortable in the beginning because I didn't know Billy all too well. We started watching a movie and things were fine. Billy started making moves on me and I kept telling him that's not what I wanted to do. He proceeded to undress me and I kept telling him "no". Billy inserted himself inside of me and then said, "You're saying no, but you know you want this". All the rest of it was a blur besides Billy telling me that, "I liked it". After Billy was done, I just laid there. I remember thinking to myself, "I didn't want to have sex". After a while, I just went to sleep. The next day, Billy took me home. I'll never forget that day because I lost my phone. I beat myself up about losing my phone and came to the conclusion that that was my punishment for going to Billy's in the first place. Even after what I had just experienced, I still found a way to blame myself for what had just taken place the night before. Crazy how we process things after being raped. In my mind, what happened between Billy and me was not rape. It did not click for me until I told a friend about what happened years later. My friend was like, "You know that's rape, right"? I was confused and in shock. Was I just that in denial? Was that behavior something that was normal to me and I was used to it? I believe the answer here is yes, to both questions.

Reflections

The summation of my sexual experiences from childhood into early adulthood changed my life drastically: the way I viewed myself, what I believed about myself, and how I interacted with others. There is one thing that all of these experiences have in common: I was not given a choice in whether I wanted to participate or not; and because my choice was taken away from me, my voice was silenced. No choice. No voice. How does one act when they think that their voice doesn't matter? This answer very well may differ from person to person, but I want to share with you how this belief manifested itself in my life.

With every experience of molestation, I fell deeper and deeper into this idea that my voice didn't matter. Imagine a nail being hammered into a slab of wood. The nail was me and my true identity, and the hammer was my life experiences. With every blow, less and less of my original design in God was present. With every blow, I fell further and further into this woman that believed that she wasn't important. I was the woman who always found herself helping others to keep her mind off of the deep issues of her heart. I was the woman who put everyone else before herself and would feel selfish for putting herself first. I was the woman who swallowed her desires to keep the peace. I was the woman who ignored how she really felt because life was easier to process that way. That woman was me. I could sit here and list out many more ways in which I related to myself as being unimportant, but the point I want you all to understand is that this thing leaks into *every* area of your life. It doesn't just stay in the bedroom or wherever you experienced the encounter. I want to challenge you all to think about how these experiences have influenced multiple areas of yourself, so I will leave reflection questions for you all to think about:

- How have my sexual experiences shaped who I am?
- What have my sexual experiences communicated to me?
- In what areas of my life do I see my sexual experiences leaking into?

- What negative things did I start to say about myself as a result of experiencing sexual assault?

I only recently began to speak out about my molestation and assault. As mentioned in the previous chapter, this idea of "sex is a secret" influenced the way I interacted with all things of a sexual nature. I never told anyone until I was older and understood the toxicity of my viewpoint and how it was stifling me. Hear me and hear me clearly: God did not create sex to be something used to belittle other people. God designed sex to be enjoyed and sex is good. Also know that your voice deserves to and needs to be heard!

Lord, I pray that you begin to heal me in those areas where I am broken. Lord, bring me to a greater understanding of who I am and why I am the way that I am. Allow me to find my voice in you and to tell my story, Lord. In Jesus' name I pray, Amen.

Journal

Journal

Journal

Journal

Journal

Journal

Journal

CHAPTER 4

Don't Touch Me

As someone who has lived through sexual assault, I have become keener in discerning behaviors, mannerisms, and the like that are "tell-tell" signs of someone who has also been assaulted. In my career, as a psychotherapist, I talk with a lot of women who have been sexually assaulted. It is very alarming to know that many of these women are unaware of the effects of experiencing such tragedies. To no surprise, I was one of these women. I, too, walked around for years not knowing how my sexual encounters had shaped me and how they had affected me. In this chapter, I discuss how my experiences with sexual assault shaped how I interacted with the world around me.

My Trauma Box

In my therapeutic work with my clients who have experienced some type of sexual trauma, I like to use what I call the "trauma box". The "trauma box" is a concept that I utilize to systematically approach trauma. As I mentioned in the previous chapter, sexual trauma does not stay in the bedroom, it leaks into many other areas of our lives. It is my job as a therapist to discover the places in which the trauma is affecting my client. To do this, I have to examine the contents that are inside of the box, one by one. The components of the box are separated into five categories: physical, mental, emotional, verbal, and spiritual. While sifting through the items in the box, the client begins to take on a new understanding of their experiences. In the next few sections, I give my account of each of these aspects and how my trauma affected me.

Physical

Before I was sexually assaulted, I did not think much about this idea of being touched. As a matter of a fact, I loved being touched and enjoyed it very much. I loved to cuddle, kiss, be rubbed on, and all the like.

After experiencing my trauma, I struggled a great deal with the idea of physical touch. I remember multiple times when people would hug me, and in the midst of the hug, their hand would gently swipe my back. My body would swiftly tense up. I never knew why my body would react in that way. If I didn't anticipate a touch coming, it would make me feel uncomfortable and as if someone was trying to take advantage of me. After I was assaulted, I also stopped going to the opposite sex's apartments and stopped allowing guys to visit mine. I had extreme trust issues and I did not trust any guy's intentions. I stayed in this phase for about three years where I did not feel safe to let anyone into my space or to leave my own space.

Self-soothing. Physically, I was in a place that I just did not trust anyone. Not realizing that I felt betrayed by God, I took it upon myself to "save myself". Little did I know, I couldn't save myself. I could only provide temporary fixes. Whenever I felt anxious or alone, I would masturbate. After all, I knew how I wanted to be touched, I knew when I was feeling uncomfortable or not, and I knew how to please myself. Before I knew it,

I was masturbating 4-5 times a day. I was addicted to making myself feel good and not depending on anyone else to do so. Some of you may be in this place, and let me forewarn you: If you are soothing/comforting yourself, you leave no room for God to do so. God wants you to trust that he can soothe you and comfort you. Let Him.

Self-punishing. Once I became comfortable, which I discuss in the next chapter, I started having sex again. Even though I knew it was wrong, I divulged. It was almost as if I couldn't control myself. At this point, I still felt convicted by the Lord for my actions. So much so, that I began to punish myself for the sins that I committed. I would force myself to not take a shower for days sometimes, just to stay in the filth of my sin. I looked at myself almost in the sense of how owners treat dogs to train them. When a dog potties somewhere it's not supposed to, the owner rubs the dog's nose in the poop and then chastises the dog to let them know that pooping is not okay in that area. To try to teach myself a lesson and to try to get myself to stop having sex, I would wallow in the filth of my sin. Who are we to punish ourselves? God does not treat us like that, so why should we? We need to give ourselves grace and mercy because God does. God does not make us stay in our filth, so neither should we.

Mental

This aspect of the trauma box was the most difficult for me to become aware of. After I was assaulted, my mind automatically shifted into survival mode. I made sure to do any and everything to protect me and my body. From a mental standpoint, I found myself overthinking the smallest of social cues. I like to call it the "deciding of good and bad touch". Every time someone touched me, my mind would unconsciously assume that it was a bad touch. What once was first nature with being touched became something that I had to sift through to figure out what it meant for me.

I also struggled heavily with how I viewed myself. My self-worth had plummeted and I didn't even realize it. I always wondered how my assailant viewed me and how they rationalized the situation to think that it was okay to assault me. My wonderings always led me to one conclusion: my assailant viewed me as worthless and as if I did not matter. That is the only possible way that I could make sense of the experience to understand why someone would do that to me. So, that's what I started to believe about myself. I started to believe that I was worthless. How does someone treat themselves if they think they are worthless? Well, for me, I always aimed low. I didn't think I deserved good things, so I went for the easy things. That applied to my relationships, my job choices, my finances, etc. Also, making decisions from the mindset of being worthless, led me to make some pretty bad decisions. I hurt a lot of people and even myself. I began to believe that because I had hurt so many people and done so much wrong, that I did not deserve to be happy. We deserve to be happy, ladies. God desires for us to live lives that are fulfilling and we are the apple of His eye. You are important. You are worthy.

Emotional

Being sexually assaulted created a moment in which I felt the most unsafe that I've ever felt in my life. As women, it is important for us to feel safe: emotionally, spiritually, physically, and mentally. With my safety being exploited, I made it my mission to protect myself in every way that I could. After my assault, I emotionally "played it safe". I did not expose myself to situations in which I could possibly lose my emotional composure. I presented myself as this well "put together" person all the time. I would get so upset if I showed any type of emotions other than happiness and self-control. It felt weak for me to show discomposure of any nature. I didn't understand how emotionally unhealthy it was for me to hoard all of my emotions and act as if they didn't exist.

Verbal

I know some of you are wondering why this is even a category that I am discussing. However, allow me to explain. During my assault, like a lot of other victims, I verbally told my assailant "no". I told him multiple times, out of my mouth, that I did not want to have sex. Did he listen? No, he did not. If someone dismisses the words that come out of your mouth, what does that make you believe about the words you have to say? For me, it made me believe that my words didn't matter. It made me believe that my voice didn't matter.

I remember the very day that I became aware of the verbal effects of my assault. I was laying in bed scrolling through my phone when my little brother entered the room. He had a towel in his hand and was twisting it up and hitting me with it, multiple times. He was, clearly, in a playful mood, but I wasn't. So, I told him, "You better not hit me in the face with that". What does he proceed to do? Hit me in the face, on purpose. My response to my brother? I threw a chair at him. A little over the top, wouldn't you say? At that moment, I didn't understand why I got so upset with him. After a little self-reflection, I realized that I had gotten so upset with my brother because he had done exactly what my assailant did: ignored my voice.

Spiritual

Spiritually, it took me a little longer to see the effects. At the time that I was assaulted, I wasn't really taking my relationship with God seriously. Therefore, when it happened, I didn't connect it back to God. I blamed myself. I wholeheartedly believed that what had happened to me was because I deserved it. Once I began to grow in my relationship with the Lord, my perception began to change. I began to question God. Why would God allow this to happen to me? Did I deserve what happened? Did it mean that I was a bad person? Did it mean that God didn't love me? Did it mean that I was unredeemable? I had *so* many questions! A lot of you may feel like God has abandoned you or that God was not with you when you were assaulted. It's a lie. God has been with you every step of the way, and if you are reading this, that means He is still with you seeing you through. You are not alone.

Reflections

What I've come to understand about my experience, over time, is that God will use some of our worst moments to show us that we are more than victims, but that we are *victors*! Just think about it: if I wouldn't have survived my assault, that would have meant that it defeated me. However, I am sitting here on the other side of the assault writing about how I made it through! What an awesome God we serve. I would not have been able to share my testimony if God wouldn't have brought me through. God used my experience with sexual assault to show that He is a healer and also to give me my testimony. Again, tell your testimonies, ladies.

I wanted to take a full chapter to explore triggers and responses so that you all can be aware of yourself. The devil's way of keeping us stuck in a situation is to keep us from the knowledge about a thing. We are no longer using "I don't know" and "I don't know how" as an excuse to keep us bound and unhealed. I challenge each and every one of you to do a deep self-reflection about your life and those moments where you may have overreacted and not quite understood why. I'll leave you with a few questions to do so:

- In what ways have I noticed that my assault has changed me *physically*?
- In what ways have I noticed that my assault has changed me *mentally*?
- In what ways have I noticed that my assault has changed me emotionally?
- In what ways have I noticed that my assault has changed me *verbally*?

- In what ways have I noticed that my assault has changed me *spiritually*?

- When I think back on situations where I 'overreacted', was it out of response to being triggered to some deeper problem that I was not aware of?

- Is this work that I can do on my own or do I need to seek professional help?

Once you figure out your triggers, you can begin to train your mind to respond to them differently and in a more healthy way. For sexual assault victims, a lot of this process looks like telling yourself, "I am not in danger. I am safe. Therefore, I do not have to respond like I usually do". Begin to think about how you would respond to triggers differently if you felt safe or if you were healed.

Lord, I pray to you right now and ask you to heal like only you know how. You see me where I am hurting. Allow me to surrender my heart to you so that you can sift through it and heal me piece by piece. Send me healing in my body, mind, emotions, voice, and my relationship with you. Lord, give me the confidence and the faith to know that I am not broken, but that I am healing. In Jesus' name I pray, Amen.

Journal

Journal

Journal

Journal

Journal

Journal

Journal

CHAPTER 5

Leverage

to use (something) to maximum advantage

In the last chapter, I explored how my trauma affected me and how it leaked into many areas of my life. As I reflected over my young adult years, I couldn't believe how much I had ignored the pain and how comfortable I had become in dysfunction. Even as painful as all of it was, I was still oblivious to the root cause of my pain or the root cause of my issue: sex had become a part of the foundation of who I was. It was the way that I found value and the thing that I used to get what I wanted.

Faulty Foundation

Imagine a house. At the foundation, the thing in which the house stands on, is sex. Everything that was built upon this foundation of sex is grown from the root of sex. What types of things get birthed from a foundation of sex? For me, it was lust, sin, fornication, adultery, homosexuality, incest, etc. When I was sexually assaulted, this house got knocked down. I no longer enjoyed sex and did not want to do it. I stopped having sex for three years and I didn't let any men come see me and I wouldn't go and visit them. What I didn't realize is that my foundation was still in place. The sex was still there, and during those three years that I stopped having sex, I rebuilt my life back upon this same faulty foundation. Why didn't I realize that sex was still there? Why didn't I understand that just because I stopped having sex that it didn't mean that I had addressed the heart of the issue? As Christians, I think we can often get preoccupied with looking at the sin we suffer with and sometimes that's all that we can see. I was so focused on the fact that I had stopped having sex that I didn't stop to think about why I was even doing it in the first place. I didn't address the real issue, so the issue persisted, even after three whole years of not having sex.

Two Peas in a Pod

Sex had become a part of who I was. If I was not having sex, I did not feel valuable. You may be wondering how sex became a part of my foundation. It was a process that began from my very first sexual encounter and continued to slowly chip away at the original foundation that was supposed to be in place. The objectification of women taught me that my body was powerful. When I realized that my body was powerful, I quickly learned that I could use my body to get what I wanted. So, that's what I started to do.

I haven't always considered myself to be the prettiest of people. In middle school, I never really dated and I blamed it on the fact that I didn't think I was pretty. When I got to high school, it was no different. I didn't take an interest in dating because no one took interest in me. When guys did take a liking to me, it wouldn't last long. As soon as they would discover that I was a virgin, they would avoid me and say things like, "Oh, you're a good girl. I can't mess with you". In my mind, I got ranked lower on this imaginary scale just because I wasn't having sex. So, if being a virgin was at the bottom of this scale, that meant that not being a virgin was at the top of this scale (or at least that's what I told myself). Oh, how I wish that I had someone to tell me that holding on to my virginity was more valuable than what some schoolboy(s) had to say! Below I give examples of how I or the people around me have used sex/sexual things to get what they want (leverage):

- My toxic relationship with sex started out simple. In high school, boys would ask me for nude pictures, and in the beginning, I refused. However, with the right words and charisma, I gave in and started to send nudes of myself to get *attention*.

- From nudes, it went to being fingered at a birthday party that I attended. Let me add here that I did not give this guy permission to do this and I didn't want it to happen. Did I tell anyone? No, not until a rumor got spread around school that I had had sex with this guy. My older sister attended the same school as me, so she heard the rumor. I had to explain myself. My options were to get lied on about having sex or tell the truth and take the chance of getting a lesser punishment. So, I told the truth. In short, I got threatened by my grandmother that she would beat me with a baseball bat if anything happened like that again. This response from my grandmother left a bad taste in my mouth. If telling the truth got me threatened, then I didn't want to speak. So, I vowed to keep everything a secret. In this scenario, sex was used for *bragging rights*.

- Fast forward to a couple of weeks before I went off to college, I decided to lose my virginity. Not because I wanted to, but because I got tired of being asked to have sex by the guy that I was dating and I got tired of telling him "no". So, sex was used to *get him off of my case* and to get him to stop asking me.

- During my three-year hiatus of not having sex, I struggled with trusting people and their intentions. I met this one guy who was really nice, cool, and down to earth. We had been friends for like a year, so I had learned a lot about him and the way he carried himself. We were hanging out one day and things started to progress. The guy knew that I hadn't had sex in three years, so he asked me if I wanted to. I told him yes because I trusted him. Sex was used to show this guy how much I really liked him and *prove to him that I trusted him.*

- As I mentioned previously, I did not think that I was a very attractive person in middle school. When I started to blossom out and "glow up", I began to recognize the power of my looks. I began to "test my limits" per se. I would go out to places and look for the guy that I found to be most attractive. If this guy gave me attention, that meant that he was interested in me. If I could get him to have sex with me, too, that meant that I was attractive. Good looking guy + sex = I'm good looking, too. Sex was used to *invalidate the insecure feelings I had about myself.*

- Old habits die hard. I met this guy and we instantly connected. I mean he literally read me my mail the first day we met. In our very first conversation, he said to me, "Lyrica, you know you don't have to have sex to feel valuable. You are worth more than that". I didn't know how to respond. It was like he had spoken to a place in me that I didn't even know existed. So, that was the start of the relationship, and even though he had said these very important words to me, they did not stick. I was so used to using sex as leverage that I did it in my relationship with a guy who truly loved and cared for me. I didn't need to manipulate him with sex to get him to care for me or to do anything for me, but I wasn't used to that. I wasn't used to someone giving me things without me having to "put out". It was a hard pill to swallow and an even harder pill to deal with. Due to other issues that came up in my relationship with this person, we broke up. I was devastated. I had invested so much into this relationship. Too much to be completely honest. I felt so lost without that relationship, and I desperately wanted it back. So, I tried to *use sex to make him stay with me*. I thought that if I "put it down right", that he would want to stay with me.

I titled this section "Two Peas in a Pod" because that is ultimately what happened. I became super acquainted with sex and did not know who I was without it. I was so deep in sin that I had become desensitized to my conviction. I no longer felt bad about having sex, and this is exactly where the devil wanted me to be, and honestly, where he wants you, too. The deeper we are in sin, the less we are able to hear God's voice and discern those things that are bad/wrong for us. Sex was a bandaid that I used to try to cover a much deeper and bigger issue: not having Christ at my foundation.

Reflections

I want to continue with the house metaphor. I have experienced two hurricanes in my life: my sexual assault and my breakup. These hurricanes tore down the very houses that I had built on my faulty foundation. How? Well, why do houses fall during hurricanes or tornadoes? Because their foundations aren't solid. God was gracious enough to send not only one hurricane, but a second one because I didn't learn my lesson the first time. God could have very well let me continue to live in my faulty foundation house, but he didn't! God cared enough to knock down what was doing me harm AND to help me rebuild a new house with Him at the foundation. I don't even want to imagine what my life would look like if God wouldn't have knocked those other houses down. I needed those hurricanes. I needed those tough seasons. I needed to feel like I lost everything. Why? So, that I could begin to live my life in a house that was meant for me! I thank God for my hurricane seasons. The bible says to count it all joy when you face trials and tribulation (James 1:2), and now I truly understand what it means. When you are walking in the will of God, EVERYTHING will work out for your good.

The biggest lesson that I've learned through my experiences is that temporary things don't fill eternal voids. You will always feel unsatisfied and unquenched when trying to solve a problem with the wrong solution. We *need* God. Only God can fill the deep wells of your heart. He is the well that never runs dry. So, I leave you with a few questions:

- What is at the foundation of my house?
- What things have I used sex for in the past or present?
- What is the thing/person/place/situation that I keep running to to try to fill an eternal void?
- What bandaid am I trying to use to cover a wound that needs more attention?

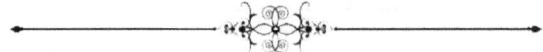

I pray, right now in the name of Jesus, that every spirit of shame is lifted off of me. I rebuke the enemy trying to whisper lies to me as I reflect on my questions. Lord, I ask that you allow me to give myself the same grace that you have given me. Allow me to begin to see me as you see me, Lord. Begin to knock down my house if it isn't built on you, so that I can live a spiritually, whole life. Allow me to forgive myself for thinking that I knew what was best for me and also for the decisions that I made during that time. I pray these things in Jesus' name, Amen.

Journal

Journal

Journal

Journal

Journal

Journal

Journal

CHAPTER 6

Who Was I Without My Pain?

[*Journal Entry*] It was as if I didn't want to heal. It was as if I wanted to stay in the pain that had haunted me for so many years. I refused to address the situation out of a fear of what would come afterward. I refused to address the situation so that my offenders could continue to live their lives comfortably. I refused to address the situation so that I wouldn't inconvenience my offenders and interrupt their lives. All the while, I was inconveniencing myself. I was suffering because I wanted to consider my offenders and their lives before my own. I was more comfortable staying in my pain because it was familiar to me instead of letting all of it go, confronting my offenders, and beginning my healing process. [*End*]

Us women are nurturers by nature. We carry children in our womb for nine months before giving birth. During these nine months, we are taking care of this child that is within us and nurturing it. Of course, children aren't the only thing that we nurture and hold on to for dear life. We nurture our pain, as well. I believed that if I held on to my pain, tightly, that I would be able to control how much of it I felt or how much it affected me. If the pain was in my hands, I knew what to expect. I couldn't even begin to fathom giving that pain to someone else and them returning it to me in worse condition than what I gave it to them in. I feared that if I said anything, it would make the situation worse. I had already dealt with so much pain on my own, that I was afraid that I would re-experience the pain if I opened my mouth about it. So, I stayed. I stayed in the pain. I stayed in the awkward interactions with my offenders. I stayed in the hurt. I stayed in the victim seat. I stayed, and I desperately did not want to be there. BUT I DIDN'T KNOW HOW TO GET OUT. That was my dilemma: where do I start? Some of you reading this may be asking yourself the same question right now. Allow me to give you some insight:

1. *Give it to God.* This may seem like a given, but it is really the most important step that you could take. So why is it so difficult for us to do this? Shame, and let me be clear, God does not make us feel ashamed. The word is very clear about those things that the Lord has come to give us (John 10:10) and shame is not one of them. So, what are you saying, Lyrica? I am saying that shame is from the devil and it is another one of his tricks to keep us stuck in a broken place. It is a plan that the devil tries to use to keep us from being healed and receiving everything that the Lord has for us. Shame makes you keep quiet about what you've experienced. Shame makes you believe that it's okay to hold on to this stuff, but it's not okay! Why? That stuff gets heavy and it will eat away at you. Silence doesn't yield healing and closed mouths don't get healed. We have to speak up. God tells us to cast our burdens upon Him because He cares for us. God wants you to give Him what burdens you, so give it to him.

2. *Get to praying.* God is our ultimate healer and we need to communicate with the one who has the power to heal us. Our time of prayer is our opportunity to ask God questions about our experiences, to ask God what the healing process looks like, and to consult with God about any fears we may have about the healing process.

3. *Go to therapy.* Yes, I am a Christian and I believe in Jesus AND a having therapist. I can not express how important it is to participate in the therapeutic experience to address all the ways that trauma affects a person. Yes, this book may have gotten a lot of you thinking about your pasts and the effects of trauma, but this book only scratches the surface of the work that is required for you to achieve your healing. So, please, please, please, go to therapy. I can hear some of you thinking now, "Well my _____ is my therapist, so I'm good". No ma'am. It is not anyone else's responsibility to heal you. It is not fair for you to put all of that on them and give them a responsibility that is not theirs. You will

burn them out. Don't do it, sis. Is it okay to talk with them about these things and make them aware of what's going on? Of course, and that's all in the right timing. However, they are not your therapist or your God.

4. *Support system.* This is where friends, family, significant others, and the like come into play. It is important to have people who can support you throughout this process. Healing from trauma can be difficult at times, and it's nice to have people there to remind you why you started in the first place, to speak life into you, and to keep your head on straight.

5. *Out with the old.* What you will start to realize during this journey is that the way you use to think and make sense of things is outdated. Kind of like spoiled milk. It no longer serves its purpose. So, you throw the milk out. There are a lot of things that you used to think that will have to be thrown out because they are no longer applicable for where you are trying to go as a healed woman. I like the way that sounds, "a

healed woman". Anywho, but we don't just throw out the old and keep it at that do we? No, of course not. Finish the saying, "in with the new". New what exactly? New thoughts about yourself. Scripture was really helpful for me during this phase. God has so many wonderful things to say about His children and His word really does an amazing job at edifying us.

6. *Address it.* Let's say someone gets cut on their arm and it damages one of the major arteries that goes to the heart. What happens if this cut isn't addressed? It continues to bleed. Some of us women have been walking around and bleeding out on everything. Why? Because we refuse to address the very thing that hurt us, the person. How can we expect to fully heal if the person that hurt us is completely unaware of the pain that they caused us? My silence and refusal to address my trauma slowly killed me for years. I had to set it free. If your offender has passed away, I encourage you to write a letter to that person and express everything about that

experience and how it made you feel, and how it has affected you. You will find so much freedom in just letting it be known.

I had become so comfortable with my pain that it was as if it was almost a part of who I was. I held on to my pain, so tightly, because I did not know what stood on the other side of me letting that pain go. I was afraid that I would feel empty without my pain. However, by hoarding this pain, I created more pain for myself. Why is it that we hold on and hide these painful experiences? Holding on to them doesn't' make us feel them any less. Actually, I think it amplifies it. We can't hold on to what we want God to heal.

Reflections

Ladies, it is not fair for us to continue to hold on to the pain that other people have caused us. It is so harmful to our mental, physical, emotional, and spiritual health. Holding on to our pain is like grasping broken glass in our hand: the tighter you squeeze, the more damage you cause yourself. We have to begin to let these things go and process them. I know some of you are wondering how to do this, but it will definitely be discussed in the next chapter. I just want to take the time to focus on and tease out this pain factor. Here are some questions:

- Have I been hoarding my pain? If so, for how long?
- Who am I without my pain?
- How has holding on to my pain affected my relationships, family, healing, etc?
- What barriers are currently standing in the way of letting go of my pain?
- Have I given my pain to God or have I been trying to manage it on my own?
- What are some old ways of thinking that I need to get rid of?
- What are some new truths that I can start speaking over myself?
- What does God say about me?
- In what ways, if any, have I started addressing my pain and wounds?

- *Journal prompt*: Take some time to freely and openly write about all of your pain. Turn on some good gospel music and let it all out!

In our healing, we have to put ourselves first. We cannot be concerned with how our healing is going to make others feel or what others will think. Your healing is not only for you but for the generations that come behind you. You are healing so that your children do not have to experience the same things that you had to go through. You are healing so that your relationships will begin to flourish. You are healing because you deserve to be whole. It's time to heal, woman of God.

Reclaiming Womanhood

Lord, I come to you right now just thanking you for who you are. I want to thank you for the beautiful woman that I am. See me, Lord. Go to those places I have hidden from you and begin to pour your love into all the cracks of my heart, soul, and mind. Allow me to release the pain I have been holding on to out of the fear that I will not know who I am without it. Lord, begin to speak your affirmations over my life and begin to whisper sweet truths to me about who I am as your daughter. I don't want to hold on to my pain anymore. Take it away from me, Lord. It's too heavy for me to carry. I know that all things work together for my good and you will use my pain for my good. I may not be able to see it now, but it will turn out for good! Lord, I thank you for all you are doing in my life and the healing you have prompted in my life. In Jesus' name I pray, Amen.

Journal

Journal

Journal

Journal

Journal

Journal

Journal

CHAPTER 7

A Flame in the Closet

Healing. The process of making or becoming sound or healthy again.

You need to heal. Healing is so important. Healing this, healing that. Heal, heal, heal. We hear things like this all the time. Healing is the new black. Talk of healing and being whole is literally everywhere you turn. So much so that everyone wants it, and rightfully so. No one wants to walk around broken, busted, and disgusted. Healing is a term we use so often, but yet most people don't know what it entails or where to even begin. I thought that I reached my healing by deciding to not have sex. Boy, was I in for a rude awakening when I realized that that was not what healing was. So, I have come to debunk all the false ideas about healing and what it looks like and to give you a practical example of how to begin that process and how to continue to walk in it.

The Flame

Imagine taking a match and striking it against a surface to light it. Now, you have a tiny flame. What does this flame represent? This flame represents anything about yourself that you typically hide from others, things that you are ashamed of, things that you try to ignore, negative thoughts/feelings that you don't want to have, the pain that you have experienced, etc. The flame resembles those things that we just don't want to deal with.

The Closet

You take this match and you throw it into your closet at your house. This action represents you ignoring whatever it is you are experiencing. This is where those destructive habits come into play. What things do you do to distract you from those things that you don't want to deal with? Bury yourself in your work, drink, smoke, have sex, put yourself in compromising situations?

The Exit

After you throw your lit match into the closet, you leave your house. This action represents you running away from the issues that you are facing. You go about your life as "normal" and try to ignore this flame that you just left at your house. You go hang out with friends, go shopping, post encouraging things on your social media, counsel your friends about their relationships, help people with their problems, etc. All the while, you are ignoring your issues.

The Return

You return to your house after "living your life" and what does your house look like? You guessed it! Your entire house is burned down. Completely destroyed. What started out as a small flame turned into a house fire and consumed literally everything.

The Secret

Too many times, because we don't want to deal with the issues we have going on, we run from them. We partake in self-destructive behaviors to try to avoid dealing with the real issues of our hearts. We distract ourselves with everyone else's problems to keep us from having to deal with ours, and by the time that we actually realize it, our problems have consumed everything in our lives. The problem is not just in your relationship with yourself, but it is now showing up in your relationship with your friends, your significant other, your family, your job, your finances, etc. Everywhere you turn, your problem is showing up. But why? When we try to ignore the issues that we have going, like the flame, they get a lot bigger. Your house is on fire. It's burning, sis.

Some of us feel like we are inside the houses as they burn down, some of us are watching the house burn down, and some of us are trying to put the fire out and save the house. Whatever position you find yourself in, they all feel pretty helpless. So, what's the alternative? How do we keep our houses from catching on fire? Those are both great questions. However, I think it's worth mentioning here, that if your house is on fire, then that probably means that it needs to be burned down. *Needs* to be burned down? Yes, God wants to make room to create a new identity in you: the one you were created to walk in all along, as His daughter.

So, in the scenario with the flame in the closet, what could have been done differently to change the outcome of the situation? One could sit with the flame until it goes out, one could blow the flame out, one could use the match to light a candle, etc. I feel like there are multiple ways of approaching this flame. What do these other approaches look like, realistically? It looks like sitting with the thing that you are running from. It looks like thinking about your feelings associated with this thing that you are ashamed of. Here are some questions to help you to begin to sit with those things that you have been running from (These will serve as the reflection questions for this chapter, so grab your journal and get to writing!):

- What have I been running from?
- What self-destructive behaviors have I been doing to distract myself from my problems?
- When I run from my problems, what do I run to?

- When I think about what I've been running from, what feelings do I experience?
- Why do I feel this way towards this situation?
- Who has contributed to me feeling this way?
- What thoughts do I have about these things that I have been running from?
- Where do these thoughts come from?
- What people have I been avoiding as a result of not addressing my issues?
- What things can I do to turn my pain, shame, hurt, anger, anxiety, etc into something productive?
- Is there someone that can help me sit with the things that I am ashamed of?
- Has God given me instructions on how to address these things and I have just been ignoring them?
- What would make it easier for me to address these things that I need to deal with?

- What is standing in the way of me addressing them?

Sitting in the pain, the disappointment, the shame, the guilt, etc can seem pretty daunting. That is why it is so important that we don't let what we see in front of us, affect our view on God and what He has promised us in His word. It is important that we speak life over ourselves in the midst of those times where we feel like the world is crumbling around us. So, how can we create or find peace in an atmosphere that is literally on fire? How can we remain calm, even though what we see in front of us is wasting away? I'm so glad you asked. We can find peace in knowing that God works everything out for our good. We can find peace in knowing that God won't leave us without a place to call home, but that He will restore what is lost. We can find peace in knowing that we are not alone and that God is with us all the way: from the flame to the house fire. We can find peace in knowing that once we come out on the other side, we won't look or smell like what we have been through. People will look at you and not even be able to tell that you have experienced such a traumatic experience. We can find peace in knowing that the grace of God does not count us out!

Reflections

Ladies, we have to start dealing with these things that have happened to us. We have to start addressing the trauma that we have experienced. The key to doing these things is being vulnerable. It wasn't until I was honest and vulnerable with myself, that I started to heal. Vulnerability is not a weakness. The devil will trick you into thinking that opening up is the wrong thing to do, but as always, the devil is WRONG. Your house has been on fire for far too long. It's time that you allow God to remove all of the unnecessary baggage from your life so that He can give you your rightful baggage. Sis, you are carrying bags that don't even belong to you. Give them to the Father. God is wanting to get rid of the pain that you have so that He can fill you with His joy. You have been hoarding your pain, and you have left no room for the Lord to pour His joy into you. I challenge you: address the pain and then let it go. It's not yours to bear. Psalm 55:22 (NLT) encourages us to, "Give your burdens to the Lord, and he will take care of you. He will not permit the godly to slip and fall". God will take care of everything that you give Him, BUT you have to make the first move. You have to give God your burdens!

Dear Heavenly Father, I ask that you give me the courage and the strength to deal with all the traumatizing things that have happened in my past. I know that it can be scary, but you have not given me a spirit of fear. I can do anything with you by my side. I owe it to myself to be healed from these things. I deserve to be whole. I deserve to heal. I deserve to live a life where I am not constantly reliving my past. I trust your word when you say you will not allow me to slip or fall. I will surrender my hurt and pain to you, Lord so that you can take care of me. I realize that by holding on to my pain, I have been blocking you from doing your job. I let go of all of my burdens right now. I don't want them anymore. Lord, fill me with your joy. I want to feel your joy again. Lord, lead me in this process because it is new for me, but I know you will guide me through it. In Jesus' name I pray, Amen.

Journal

Journal

Journal

Journal

Journal

Journal

Journal

CHAPTER 8

What it Means to be a Woman

Identity. The fact of being who or what a person or thing is.

Throughout this book, I have spent a lot of time picking apart this idea of what it means to be a woman, where those ideas come from, and also how those beliefs manifest themselves in our actions. The way that culture defines womanhood, in a nutshell, leads us, women, to do some pretty unhealthy and broken things. That is why I have spent the majority of the book disqualifying the lies that are told to us by society. The purpose of this book was to uncover the enemy's plan to keep us women in bondage, to keep us women broken, and to keep us, women, from living out our purposes. By uncovering this information and giving you the game plan for how the devil operates, you are now in a position to fight a *prepared* battle. You will begin to see the schemes of the enemy from a mile away. Why? Because you will know what to look for. The devil has been sneak attacking your identity as a woman for far too long. We are no longer allowing a lack of knowledge to be the reason why we keep staying underneath the enemy's thumb. It is time to educate ourselves and level up. So, now that we have our knowledge and we have dismantled "worldly womanhood", it's now time to define womanhood from the eyes of our Father.

Child of God

In the introduction of the book, I illustrated, through the use of an example, the importance of knowing who your manufacturer is. God is the one who created us and called us His children. He knows us better than anyone else and even better than we know ourselves. So, it only makes sense that we consult Him when it comes to defining who we are. Before we wear any title/label, we are, first and foremost, children of God. If we don't understand our lineage as a child of God, it is more likely that we will struggle in the other areas of our lives such as wifehood, womanhood, parenthood, etc.

The more you know/seek the Father, the more you know yourself. So, if we want to discover more information about who we are, we should seek God. This is the beginning of reconstructing the foundation of our houses. This is the start of building our identity in Christ and doing away with all that the world has tried to taint us with. This idea of "seeking God" may sound a lot cliche to you and I'm almost certain that you've heard it before: "Seek the Kingdom of God above all else, and live righteously, and he will give you everything you need" (Matthew 6:33 NLT). This scripture is a very common one, and if not careful, we can miss the weight of the verse. We have to go a step further. Yes, we know to seek God, but what does that look like? How does one seek God? I've coordinated with a few of my spiritual mentors to give you a list of tips on how to seek God and how to build your identity in Christ:

- First and foremost, forgive yourself and anyone else that you need to forgive. If we have unforgiveness in our hearts, we will not be in a position to receive God and His authenticity.

- Confront the foundation of your house. If our foundation is not built on God, then it's time to start the process of breaking down the old and building up the new. We can't build our new identities on that same faulty foundation.

- Spend time with God. When we want to get to know someone, we spend time with them. It works the same way with God. No matter where you are in your walk of faith, God always wants to spend time with you.

- Talk to God. He wants to hear from you and He cares about what you have to say: from the little annoyances in your day to the big decisions you have to make.

- Read His word. God's word is where we begin to learn about His character. In any relationship, it is important to get to know more about that person: their likes, dislikes, habits, beliefs, etc. The more you know about a person, the better you are able to connect with them.

- Surround yourself with other godly women. When we are embarking on new journeys, it is important that we have people there to show us the way and to encourage us when we are feeling defeated, tired, or weary. These women will help lead you in the right direction and point you to scripture that will edify you as a woman of God.

Womanhood

Truth be told, the more that I thought about womanhood, the less I seemed to grasp the concept of it. Understanding womanhood is almost like pulling at a loose thread from a t-shirt: the more you pull, the more entangled you become. This isn't necessarily a bad thing. It just means that womanhood isn't a one size fits all definition, and that's okay. To be a woman means many things. Women are multifaceted beings.

There is a lot that can be pulled from scripture about who a woman is. The scripture that a lot of women look to is Proverbs 31 (P31). This scripture gives an account of a woman/wife who seemingly has it all figured out and has it all together. The P31 woman is painted to be this perfect woman, and if not careful, we will begin to strive for perfection. What's wrong with that? None of us are perfect and we are all bound to make mistakes. So, what ends up happening is we, women, begin to feel like a failure because we feel as if we don't measure up to the perfect life of the P31 woman. We weren't created to be perfect. God made you and created you for a specific purpose with all of your imperfections in mind. So, the question becomes: Why should we look to the P31 woman to give us information about womanhood? Because it gives us something to strive towards and it also gives us a framework to operate from. Without this framework, we are left to define womanhood by our own definitions or no definition at all, and defining things by our own standards, is a recipe for disaster.

So, I could easily sit here and list out all the examples of the women in the Bible. I could analyze each woman, who they were, and what they brought to the table. If I were to do that, what would I be presenting you with that would be different from what you have already tried? Absolutely nothing. Why? Because being a woman of God is more than just reading a bunch of scriptures. Some of you can testify to the fact that simply reading scripture, is not the answer to all our problems. So, what is? The answer is simple: discovery. Womanhood is about discovering who you are. Most of the memorable women in the Bible are remembered for a specific thing that they did. This list of things includes being a ruler of armies, a protector, an innovator, a disciple, a wise person, etc. The list goes on. These women knew their purpose and operated in it to their full capacity. They weren't concerned with trying to be a perfect woman or a woman who was able to do all things. They did what they were called to do, and they did a good job of it. If they had not been in the right position to hear from God, they would have missed the opportunity to be who God called them to be. Don't miss out on your purpose trying to be something that you are not or trying to be someone that God has not called you to be.

Reflections

We are all uniquely made and handpicked for a specific purpose. We all possess certain qualities about ourselves that God hand-picked for us to have. I cannot stress enough how important it is to know God and to seek Him concerning who you are as a woman and what He wants you to carry out for His Kingdom. With that being said, I want to encourage you to get before the Lord and to ask Him what it is that He desires for you as a woman of God. Only He can tell you. I could tell you all what it means, to me, to be a woman, but that may not apply to you. I would, then, be doing you all a disservice, and that is not what I want to do. I only wish to help you reclaim your rightful position as a woman and to take back everything that the enemy has stolen from you.

If you have made it to this point in the book, I can only imagine what you may be feeling. I applaud you for sticking with it and finishing the journey. I know it may not have always been easy. This is only the beginning. Continue to discover the woman who God has created you to be. It is so worth it and I am a living testament of that. There is hope for you and your story. God is a redeemer and He will redeem you. You just have to allow Him. With the book coming to a close, I want to leave you all with a piece of wisdom from a dear friend of mine. God has called us to be the light of the world, and writing this book has allowed me to shine *my* light. So, to all of you who are reading this: Find *your* light and let it shine!

You are the light of the world -- like a city on a hilltop that cannot be hidden. No one lights a lamp and then puts it under a basket. Instead, a lamp is placed on a stand, where it gives light to everyone in the house. In the same way, let your good deeds shine out for all to see, so that everyone will praise your heavenly Father. (Matthew 5:14-16)

125

Become a Member of the Community!

Reclaiming Womanhood has an exclusive, private Facebook group where women who have been sexually assaulted can have a safe space to process and heal. I would love for you to be a part of the community. Scan the code below to get access to the group. Can't wait to see you there!

Work Cited

Department of Justice, Office of Justice Programs, Bureau of Justice Statistics, Sexual Assault of Young Children as Reported to Law Enforcement (2000).

Department of Justice, Office of Justice Programs, Bureau of Justice Statistics, Sex Offenses and Offenders (1997).

www.ingramcontent.com/pod-product-compliance
Lightning Source LLC
Chambersburg PA
CBHW051945160426
43198CB00013B/2305